To

Eileen & Neal.

Happy Anniversary

Your Friend

Lawrence Welk

W9-BMB-759

Books by Lawrence Welk with Bernice McGeehan
WUNNERFUL, WUNNERFUL!
AH-ONE, AH-TWO!
MY AMERICA, YOUR AMERICA

Lawrence Welk's Musical Family Album

Lawrence Welk
with Bernice McGeehan

PRENTICE-HALL, INC.
Englewood Cliffs, New Jersey

Lawrence Welk's Musical Family Album
by Lawrence Welk with Bernice McGeehan

Copyright © 1977 by Lawrence Welk

All rights reserved. No part of this book may be
reproduced in any form or by any means, except
for the inclusion of brief quotations in a review,
without permission in writing from the publisher.

Printed in the United States of America

Design and Art Direction: Hal Siegel
Production Editor: Shirley Stein

Unless otherwise credited, all pictures are from
the personal files of the artists involved, or the
files of Don Fedderson Productions and/or
Teleklew.

Prentice-Hall International, Inc., London
Prentice-Hall of Australia, Pty. Ltd., Sydney
Prentice-Hall of Canada, Ltd., Toronto
Prentice-Hall of India Private Ltd., New Delhi
Prentice-Hall of Japan, Inc., Tokyo
Prentice-Hall of Southeast Asia Pte. Ltd., Singapore
Whitehall Books Limited, Wellington, New Zealand

10 9 8 7 6 5 4 3 2 1

Library of Congress Cataloging in Publication Data

Welk, Lawrence.
   Lawrence Welk's Musical family album.

   1. Welk, Lawrence   —Portraits, etc.
2. Music, Popular (Songs, etc.)—United States—
Pictorial works.   I. McGeehan, Bernice.   II. Title.
III. Title: Musical family album.
ML422.W33A277   780'.42   77-24935
ISBN 0-13-526624-6

Dear Friends + Fans,

IT is my fervent hope that this Picture album of my Musical Family will help you get to know us a little better, + bring you Some Pleasant Memories as you thumb through its Pages.

With affection + gratitude to you, our loyal Audience.

Lawrence

FOREWORD

I've always loved my work. Making music, trying to please our audiences, finding and developing new talent—all these have given me tremendous joy. My life has seemed complete. And yet, just a few years ago (and to my vast surprise!), I found myself involved in yet another career, writing books with the help of my wonderful co-author, Bernice McGeehan, and this too, has given me great joy. I've written three books in the past seven years, and all of them have been so well accepted by our loyal fans, it has been extremely gratifying to me. I'm always on the lookout for something I think may be of interest to them.

So when the idea for this picture album was first suggested to me, I felt it would be something our fans could truly enjoy—but I was afraid I wouldn't be able to do it! That's because I was caught in an enormously heavy schedule at the time—taping our television show, preparing the Tahoe show, and getting ready to go on the road. With a schedule like that, I knew I'd never be able to devote enough time to a project as important as a picture album of my very own Musical Family! That's when Bernice came to my rescue. She offered to take over the major portion of responsibility herself, and because I knew how dedicated she is to anything we undertake, I agreed to go ahead. I knew I could rely on her.

Normally, Bernice and I share the amount of work that goes into each of my books, but let me say right now that on this one—she did all the work! Or most of it, anyway. After she finished the preliminary work and research, we got together and spent several weeks during which I sifted through the pictures and made final selections. Then I talked candidly about each person and each picture you'll see in this book. And everything you read comes straight from my heart.

I feel deeply indebted to Bernice for her tremendous help. I've often felt the Good Lord has had His arms around me when He guided certain people into my life or my Musical

Family, and I certainly feel that way about her! And both Bernice and I are indebted to the wonderful friends and co-workers who helped make this book possible. The girls in our office, Julie Jobe, Laurie Rector, Barbara Curtiss and Margaret Heron were all outstandingly helpful in tracking down pictures and people, and Margaret, in particular, did a superb job handling all the mail. Les Kaufman, head of our public relations staff, contributed the expertise of his years in the business. Chris Hamilton and my son, Larry Welk, Jr., of Ranwood Records spent hours helping us find exactly the right picture. Ted Lennon stood by, always ready to lend a hand or encouragement. Even my managers Sam Lutz and Don Fedderson got into the act with suggestions and advice!

My pal Eddie Shipstad not only lent us pictures from his personal files, but took special shots just for this book. Hal Siegel, Art Director for Prentice-Hall, personally flew out to confer with us, and worked long and hard to produce the kind of book we felt our fans would enjoy.

Finally, the "kids" in our Musical Family helped by looking through their own albums to find pictures that would be just right for this one. To each and every one of these wonderful people go my deepest, warmest thanks.

But most of all my thanks go to you, our readers and fans. You are the ones who have made our Musical Family possible—and we all thank you.

I was very pleased when Prentice-Hall asked me to do a family album for our fans and friends, because the idea of "family" life itself has always been so important to me. I've been a lucky man in that respect—enjoying a wonderful and warm childhood on our family farm-home near Strasburg, North Dakota; then an equally happy home life with my wife, Fern, our three children, and ten grandchildren; and finally, my unique and wonderful relationship with our Musical Family of today, many of whom have been with me so long, they're just like my own children.

My journey through life has been long—and happy! I've dreamt great dreams and been fortunate enough to see most of them come true. But never in my wildest dreams did I ever imagine I'd become the "father" to fifty children! And sometimes I ask myself—how in the world did this happen? How did I ever go from a two-piece band (me and a drummer!) to our great big fifty-member organization of today? If you'd like to find out how it happened, then come along with me now as I look back over the years—and let's see how it all got started!

Lee Rodriguez Photography, Houston, Texas

This is where it all began, on a small farm near Strasburg, North Dakota, where I was born March 11, 1903, to my parents, Ludwig and Christina Schwahn Welk—the sixth of eight children. My parents were German immigrants, who came to this country from Alsace-Lorraine via Odessa, Russia, and they brought with them nothing but their prayer books, their high hopes, their utter belief in freedom and democracy— and, oh yes, my father's antique button accordion! It was enough.

I think you can tell, from the twinkle in my father's eyes, what a wonderful sense of humor he had. He was a great tease, and loved to play little jokes on us children—a trait I seem to have inherited from him, according to my own children!

It's probably a good thing he had a sense of humor—at least where I was concerned—because I couldn't seem to do anything right. I disliked milking cows, for example, so I tried to make it more interesting by milking in rhythm. But the cows didn't like it, and they retaliated by kicking over the milk pail, or flicking a tail across my face. When I tried to pump the bellows on Father's blacksmith forge, I couldn't seem to get that right either, and Father would frequently explode in exasperation, crying *"Dummer Esel!* Can't you do *anything* right?" And when it came to butchering the hogs—well, little Lawrence was nowhere to be found! As a farmer, I was a complete washout.

In desperation, Father gave up trying to make a farmer out of me and advanced me four hundred dollars to buy a truly fine piano accordion. In return, I promised to stay on the farm four more years, and turn over to him all the money I made playing for barn dances and wedding parties.

I've always been very grateful for his decision, because I know how very worried he was for fear I'd lose my faith, in the rough and tumble world of show business.

As it turned out, however, he and my mother had instilled such bone-deep religious faith into me, that it never deserted me. And it is with me still, to this day.

It's difficult for me to speak of my mother, even today, without getting a lump in my throat, or a mist in my eyes, because to me, she was the loveliest of ladies . . . so kind, so compassionate, so understanding, that I can never recall her saying a cross word to anyone—not even us children. If we did misbehave, she never scolded. Instead, her blue eyes would look as if they were about to fill with tears—and I would have done almost anything to avoid that!

She had a lovely voice, and led us in song when we gathered round the family pump organ in the evening. She was a fine dancer, too, and taught me to waltz while my father played the accordion and my brother John the clarinet. (Years later, when I came home to

Strasburg with my little orchestra, I'd always step down off the bandstand so she and I could have a waltz together.) I believe the reason I love to dance so much today is because she taught me when I was so young.

I thought of her then—and I think of her now—almost with reverence. She gave her life to us . . . giving all of us the kind of unquestioning, complete love which is strong enough to last a lifetime. Her husband, her children, her God, were her whole life, and her gentleness and goodness—her unwavering faith—made an indelible impression on me. Because of her, I have always had the highest regard for mothers, and motherhood.

Could it be that is why the mothers of America have always been our most loyal fans?

This is the only baby picture of me I've been able to find. It's probably the only one in existence, because we didn't spend much on photographers in those days. Or on anything else! Note the parasol over my baby carriage. I guess my mother didn't trust that hot Dakota summer sun! I can't recall who the people in the buggy are, at the extreme right, but that's my sister Barbara at the extreme left, then my father, then brothers Louis and John, and little Agatha in front, and my sister Ann Mary next to my mother and me. (Father built the house you see in the background. It had very thick sod walls, covered with siding, and is still standing today.)

Ss. Peter and Paul Church, around which the life of our community centered. The organist, Max Fichtner, welded the shopkeepers and farmers thereabouts into a nationally famous choir, and he was a great inspiration to me. In fact, this church, with its beautiful music and strict teachings, was a tremendous influence on my life.

Dressed in my best and ready to tackle the world! This was taken just after I left the farm on my twenty-first birthday, March 11, 1924, with just my accordion, a change of clothing, a few dollars, my prayer book —and vast enthusiasm!

With Lincoln Boulds' band in Estherville, Iowa, my first traveling band—and did I learn a lot!

You'll notice my name is spelled out in rhinestones. That's because nobody—absolutely nobody—knew who I was at the time!

George T. Kelly, the man who changed my life. He hired me for his little traveling theatrical show, The Peerless Entertainers, and taught me more about show business—and life—than anyone else, before or since. George devoted himself to my welfare, patiently helping me develop my talents and overcome my faults. He also shared his earnings with me, and his ideas became the nucleus of the family training and sharing system we use in our organization today. George's philosophy and generosity of heart have reached far beyond his scope of time and place, touching and changing the lives of the young performers on our show today, and—through them—the world. A fine man.

WELK'S NOVELTY BAND

One of my earliest bands—six pieces, counting me—performing for
our sponsors, the Gurney Seed and Nursery Company, over WNAX,
in Yankton, South Dakota, advertising hog tonic and chicken feed.
Those radio broadcasts in the mid-twenties made our name widely
known in a four-hundred-mile radius around Yankton. We became
a semi-name band overnight! Left to right are:
Paul Donnelly, Gordon Malie, Spider Webb,
Jim Garvey, me, and Rollie Chestney.

This pretty girl is Edith Frostensen.
Her brother Jack and I were good friends
and I roomed with their family in Yankton.
(How do you like the way we used to dress?)

Maxine Grey was our first girl singer. I found her at the Baker Hotel in Dallas, or rather Fern did. Fern heard her singing over radio station WFAA, liked her, called my attention to her, and together we went to the station to see her. One look—and I took her right along with the band.

Here I am in my Cord Cabriolet with front-wheel drive. I also had a seven-passenger Pierce Arrow big enough to carry the whole band, and we made quite a procession as we sailed grandly into town—Fern and I in the Cord, and the boys in the Pierce Arrow! At least we *looked* as if we were successful.

The "family" beginning to grow. Now we're up to ten pieces. This was taken during the thirties. Jerry Burke, who's at the organ, made many friends for us with his fantastic technique and "limber" fingers.

Still growing! Now we're up to fourteen pieces, playing at the beautiful Trianon Ballroom in Chicago, with cute little Jayne Walton as our Champagne Lady. Jayne could sing perfect Spanish, and contributed greatly to the success of the band with her version of "Maria Elena" in those years.

And still growing! Here we are filling in for the great Guy Lombardo at the Roosevelt Hotel in New York in 1947. I was really thrilled with our booking till opening night, when a lady waltzed by and, eyeing me through her lorgnette, inquired frostily, "What kind of music *IS* this?" "It's the Champagne Music of Lawrence Welk," I replied. "Whaaaat?" she asked, in astonishment. I repeated my statement. "Well," she said, "it's *terrible!*"

Jack Lomas

Roberta Linn sang with us when we first appeared on television in Los Angeles, playing from the Aragon Ballroom in nearby Santa Monica. She became locally famous for her pert songs and infectious giggle. Our momentous TV debut actually happened very simply. Klaus Landsberg of KTLA sent down a remote truck one night and set up cameras to televise us as we played our usual evening dance. I didn't think too much about it till next morning when I went out to play golf. At least twenty people came up to tell me they had seen us on television and planned to come down to the ballroom, to dance with us, and I realized, as never before, the tremendous potential of this powerful medium. Immediately, I set my sights on a national television show.

This is one of our early television advertisements. By now, Alice Lon had become our Champagne Lady.

At last! Our first national television show over the ABC network, July 2, 1955. A dream come true. I don't think anything will ever equal the thrill of that first broadcast. You can see the Lennon Sisters, Alice Lon, Big Tiny Little at the piano, and— up in the string section—Dick Kessner, famous for his smooth and velvety violin tone, and Aladdin, who brought us many friends with his dramatic recitations.

America's sweethearts of song, the lovely Lennon Sisters. Janet was only nine and a half years old here, when the girls made their first appearance with us. They literally grew up on the show and developed into one of the finest singing groups in the nation. We were all proud of their great progress, and it was a delight to have them on the show for twelve years.

Dodge was our wonderful sponsor both locally and nationwide for several years, and we will be forever grateful to them for having faith and giving us our start in television. Our first producer, Ed Sobol, is at the left, and next to him you can spot Jim Hobson, our producer today.

This is the Aragon, sister ballroom of the beautiful Trianon in Chicago, where we played for many years.

Alice Lon was a lovely dancer, and famous for her frilly petticoats, which her mother made for her. You can see Buddy Merrill in the background, a talented musician who started with us when he was still very young.

And still growing—a long, long way from that little five-piece group I started out with! If you look closely, you can spot Jo Ann Castle, famous for her ragtime, honky-tonk piano, and Natalie Nevins of the silvery voice, in the front row. Pretty little Barbara Boylan was Bobby Burgess' dance partner in those years, and that's Frank Scott sitting at the piano. He was with us for many years before he returned to North Dakota.

Tom Mareschal

And here we are today, fifty members strong—and still growing. I am so proud of each and every member of our family, and feel so very close to them, that I'd like to have each of you get to know them a little better, too.

Our Musical Family

NORMA ZIMMER

Norma Zimmer! Isn't she lovely? I've always said, if there's perfection in humanity—Norma certainly has it! She's just about perfect, both in her singing and her own beautiful nature, and choosing her as our Champagne Lady was one of the wisest decisions I ever made.

Those of you who've read her book, *Norma*, know what a difficult childhood she had—born into a family so poor there was sometimes no food to eat, nor enough warm clothes to wear. That kind of poverty might have destroyed some people. But not Norma! She used it as an incentive to better herself, and today she's a star, at the very peak of her profession—and even more widely loved through her appearances on various religious programs.

Leo North

But always, her family comes first. She's a devoted wife to her husband, Randy, a dedicated mother to their two sons, Ron and Mark, and an absolutely delighted first-time "grandmama" to little Kristen, daughter of Ron and Candi Zimmer, whom you see pictured with her here.

She's a lovely, lovely lady who's come a long way from the tiny town of Larsen, Idaho, where she was born on July 13, and everyone in our Musical Family is grateful that she said "Yes" when I asked her— on camera—on New Year's Eve in 1960, to be our Champagne Lady. Norma—it has been our privilege.

Tom Mareschal

JIMMY ROBERTS

When you think of Norma on our show, you automatically think of Jimmy Roberts, who often sings duets with her. "Gentleman Jim" has been with us ever since our Aragon days on Lick Pier in Santa Monica, California, and I don't know anyone who has a more even temperament —or more good friends! He's one of the nicest people I've ever met, and all the ladies love him!

 We show him here as he looks when he sings "I Left My Heart in San Francisco," which happens to be one of his most requested songs on our television show. Another trademark song for Jimmy is "My Old Kentucky Home," a natural, since his hometown is Madisonville, Kentucky.

 Jimmy was born on April 6, and joined our show in 1954.

CHARLOTTE HARRIS

Wasn't she a pretty little girl? No wonder she's so famous today. She started playing the piano when she was only three, and the cello at five, and today, with her flawless technique and superb tonal quality, she's the best argument I know for "starting young"!

Charlotte agrees with me that early training can make all the difference, and develop habits which lead to happiness and success later in life. (Well, now, how do you like this! Here I go making a speech on my favorite subject, giving young people a chance to work early in life. But Charlotte is such a beautiful example of what can happen when you start young, I decided to make my little speech right here! So, thank you, Charlotte.)

Charlotte was born April 29 in Oak Park, Illinois, and joined our orchestra in 1961, the first—and only—girl musician in the band.

ANACANI

I found this lovely little Mexican señorita in Escondido—or maybe she found me, I've never been quite sure which! I was coming out the door of our Welkome Inn Restaurant there, just as she and her family were coming in. We all stopped . . . stared . . . Anacani said, excitedly, "*There* he is!" . . . I took one look, said, "Do you sing?" . . . and a star was born!

Anacani served as our Singing Hostess at Escondido for a few months when she first began appearing on our broadcast, but she became so popular, so quickly, we had to take her away from the restaurant and keep her on the show full time. Her Spanish songs and flashing-eyed prettiness have become great favorites with our audience.

She comes from a very musical family and works constantly to improve her talents. She's learned to play the guitar, and, just recently—the accordion! (Now, there's competition I never expected!)

And fellows, this girl is not only pretty, makes her own clothes, and is a tremendous cook—she's still single! (Makes me wish I'd had another son.)

Anacani was born in a small town near Mazatlán, Mexico, on April 10, and joined our show in 1972.

Bill Harris

Tom Mareschal

Anacani with Henry Cuesta and me
on the day she made her first
appearance on our show.

Leo North

BOBBY AND CISSY

Again, here are two young people who got started at a very early age. Bobby was one of the original Mouseketeers, and Cissy started dancing almost before she could walk, and today, as I've often said on television, they are America's finest young dance couple, without question.

They have over two hundred routines in their repertoire, and when they're preparing a new number—nothing is too much trouble. Once they flew to San Francisco, just to check on the authenticity of a Greek dance they were planning to do, and other times they've consulted college professors, or cultural groups, to make sure of the same thing. They bring great artistry to our show, and complete dedication, and I absolutely treasure their loyalty and devotion.

In private life, Bobby is married to Myron Floren's pretty daughter, Kristie (now that's keeping it in the family!) and they live in a beautiful home in the Hollywood Hills with their baby daughter, Becki Jane.

Leo North

Leo North

Cissy also lives in the Hollywood Hills, but she's such a busy young lady, she's rarely home. Still single, she's not quite ready to settle down. (But fellows, she's looking!)

I told you she was born to dance!
Here's Cissy, age three,
ready for her first dance recital.

We're showing this picture of Cissy alone, because there's such a cute story behind it. When this show was being taped, Bobby was at the hospital, awaiting birth of his first-born, Becki. His wife, Kristie, tried valiantly to cooperate and have the baby before show time, but she didn't quite manage it, and when the show went on the air, Bob was still at the hospital. "Never mind!" cried Cissy, rushing on stage, "I can do this dance alone!" And here you see her dancing her "half" of their dance by herself.

Cissy was born January 3, in Albuquerque, New Mexico, and joined our Family in 1967; Bobby was born May 19, in Long Beach, California, and joined us in 1961.

ARTHUR DUNCAN

Arthur Duncan, the man who is keeping the art of tap dancing alive in this country . . . and one of the finest gentlemen I know.

He's a tremendous hit with our audiences on personal appearance tours because, in addition to his dancing talent, he's a wonderful standup comedian, with a great sense of timing and a warm, engaging personality. I want to tell you, folks—Arthur's a very hard act to follow!

He and his wife, Alicia, are very close to his brothers and sisters, and to his elderly father, who still lives in Pasadena, California, where Arthur was born September 25, one of a family of twelve children. He became a member of our Musical Family in 1964.

Tom Mareschal

TOM NETHERTON

I'm indebted to my good friends Sheila and Harold Schafer for discovering Tom for me. They hired him to sing in the show at their restored, pioneer village of Medora, North Dakota, and then began telling me how wonderful he was. "He'd be just perfect for your show!" they said. (Well, how many times have I heard *that*?) But when I went home that spring on my annual visit to North Dakota, I played a round of golf at the Apple Creek Country Club in Bismarck, and guess who "just happened" to be there? You're right, Tom Netherton, along with a piano accompanist. He sang a couple of songs for me—and I was hooked!

Tom has been so well accepted by our audience, especially by the ladies, I sometimes think every mother in the audience has a daughter just for Tom. Recently a mama stopped me and asked if I couldn't arrange for her daughter to meet him. "She's a beautiful blonde," said mama, "and she'd be just *perfect* for Tom!" (Now where have I heard THAT before!) "Well, I'm very sorry, lady," I said, "but I'm only in the orchestra business!"

Here's Tom with—surprise—his mother! Doesn't she look young? You can see where he gets his good looks.

With his rich, deep voice, Tom is truly a great addition to our
show, and an exceptionally fine young man who is a deeply committed
Christian, often singing at religious convocations all over the nation. He
has made several fine religious albums, too. It is indeed a pleasure to
have him in our Musical Family.

Tom was born January 11, in Munich, Germany, where his
father was stationed after the war. He joined our Family in 1972.

RALNA AND GUY

Ralna and Guy are one of the nicest things that ever happened to me—or maybe I should say, *two* of the nicest! When I first auditioned Ralna at our Santa Monica office, I was so thrilled by her voice I barely noticed the tall, handsome young fellow who was playing her guitar accompaniment. But after Ralna had been with us for a few months, she began telling me how talented her husband was, and finally I agreed to audition him. When he came down to the studio—it was the same young man! And when I listened to the two of them sing together, I got such a goosebump chill, I knew I'd found something very special. (I also knew how stupid I'd been not to hire Guy along with Ralna in the first place.)

I'd like to tell you folks that those looks they give each other are absolutely real. They truly do love one another and have such a beautiful home life together. I know, because recently they invited me to dinner to talk over some future professional plans, and Ralna cooked such a good meal I gained three and a half pounds!

(And spent the next week just nibbling at my food, trying to lose that extra poundage.)

Leo North

I cannot speak of Ralna without mentioning the way she sings "How Great Thou Art." That really brings out the goosebumps and—when she hits that high note at the end—usually a standing ovation from the audience, too. I think it's Ralna's own deep religious feelings which make that song such a moving experience for all of us.

Ralna was born June 19, in Spur, Texas, and joined our Family in 1969; Guy was born September 24, in Tupelo, Mississippi, and joined us in 1970.

Tom Mareschal

Ralna lost her voice temporarily due to laryngitis, and here she's "answering" Guy with a printed message!

JOE FEENEY

A couple of years ago, Joe Feeney's big number at Harrah's in Lake Tahoe was "Serenade" from *The Student Prince*. It was timed to last just long enough so I could make a quick change into a white tuxedo for a waltz number with Cissy King. But I could have taken my time, because every night I had to stand in the wings and wait while Joe took bow after bow, in front of a cheering, screaming audience. But I really didn't mind. I enjoyed Joe's thrilling Irish tenor voice just as much as they did, and joined in the applause myself.

Joe and his wife, Georgia, have quite a brood—ten children—and we can count on at least one little Feeney showing up for our Christmas broadcast every year!

Bob Ralston playing piano accompaniment for Joe.

Leo North

Here Joe and I are serenading the ladies in the audience.
Joe was born August 15, in Grand Island, Nebraska (where I played the Glovera Ballroom regularly for years and years), and joined us in 1957.

MYRON FLOREN

Right after I hired Myron Floren, I got a phone call from my manager, Sam Lutz.

"Is it true you just hired another accordion player?" he demanded.

"Yes, Sam, it is," I said, meekly.

"And is it true he plays better than you do?" he screamed, incredulously.

"Yes, Sam, I'm afraid he does."

There was a choking sound at the other end of the line. Then Sam said, "Welk—you've done a lot of dumb things in your time. But this is the worst!"

"Oh, now, Sam," I remonstrated, "it can't be as bad as that."

"Oh, no? Lawrence—let me paint you a picture. Let's say Tommy Dorsey goes on the road, and after he plays a couple of trombone solos for the audience, some young kid from the back row comes down and plays better than he does! Don't you see what you've done, Lawrence, don't you get it?"

"Yes, Sam, I get it," I told him, "but it's too late. We've already shaken hands on the deal. And in our band—that's as good as a contract!"

And I've never regretted it. (Neither has Sam, not with all those bookings that keep coming in for Myron!) Myron is not only a brilliant accordionist, he's a wonderful man, and never fails to make new friends for us on his countless personal-appearance tours. I don't know what we'd do without him.

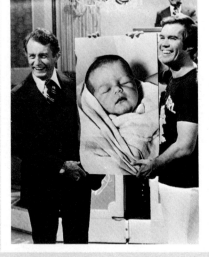

Married to Berdyne Floren, Myron has five pretty daughters, and just recently became a grandpa for the first time, courtesy of daughter Kristie and son-in-law Bobby Burgess. In fact here's a picture of Myron and Bobby displaying a giant-sized poster of Miss Becki Burgess, taken just seconds after she was born, November 17, 1976.
Myron was born November 5,
in Webster, South Dakota, and
joined us in 1950.

And here we are just after I
hired Myron, in Chicago.

HENRY CUESTA

No wonder I love my business! Every once in a while, you'll take a gamble—and hit the jackpot! That's just what happened with Henry Cuesta.

One day, a batch of records arrived in my office. They were from Henry, and when I played them, I had a hunch I'd found the clarinet man I'd been looking for. I called him immediately in Toronto, Canada, where he was working, and invited him to "join the family!" (Later, I learned Henry had sent his recordings on the advice of the late, great Bobby Hackett, who'd suggested he get in touch with our George Thow.)

And am I glad I did! Henry's not only one of the finest musicians we've ever had, he's one of the finest men I've ever known, too, with a beautiful family—very warm, very loving . . . the kind that lives and works for each other, the kind that built this country.

It's a real joy to have this dedicated and talented artist in our Musical Family.

As you can see, Henry also believes in "starting them young"! Here he is with his young son, Henry, Jr., and me, in the backyard of our home. This picture was taken by Lee Rodriguez, one of my favorite photographers.

Henry was born on December 23, in Corpus Christi, Texas, and joined us in 1972.

DICK DALE

Dick Dale is one of those all-around people so necessary to any show. He plays a fine saxophone, sings well (you see him often in duets with Gail Farrell), acts in comedy sketches (he's a terrific mimic), dances (more or less!), and has such a friendly personality that everyone likes him.

When I first found him, he was playing in Harold Loeffelmacher's Six Fat Dutchmen Old-Time Band . . . and all I can say is, Harold's loss was our gain!

Dick has been with us for twenty-six years—but hasn't aged a day.

Dick was born September 14, in Algona, Iowa, and joined us in 1951.

Leo North

AVA BARBER

When Ava Barber sent us an audition tape of her voice, I was so impressed I couldn't get it out of my mind. So a few weeks later, when I had occasion to play in a golf tournament in Nashville, Tennessee, I called Ava at her home in Knoxville, to see if she'd like to audition for me "in person." "*Would I!*" she exclaimed—or words to that effect—and sure enough, when I arrived at the tournament, Ava and her husband, Roger Sullivan, were there waiting to greet me. Ava "auditioned" for me that day by trailing me around the golf course, while Roger played a tape recording of her songs!

She has a wonderful voice—rich, warm, absolutely true—and her style with a country-music song has won her a huge following, as well as a couple of hit recordings. It's been a pure delight having this lovely Southern lady on our show.

Tom Mareschal

Doesn't she look like a real "country gal" here? Ava has a great sense of humor, by the way, and the girls tell me she keeps them in hysterics in the dressing room.

Ava was born June 28, in Knoxville, Tennessee, and joined us in 1974.

SANDI, GAIL, AND MARY LOU

Well, I could write a whole book on these lovely girls alone! They're all so very, very talented.

Sandi, as the lead singer, has that special quality in her voice that lends authority to the group, and such a warm, sweet smile! Not only that, she has the most glorious red hair I've ever seen in my lifetime, and I'm only now beginning to forgive her for cutting it off! She was in the doghouse with me for a few weeks after she cut it, but it's impossible to stay angry at such a lovely lady!

Sandi is married to Brent Griffiths, Financial Manager for Walt Disney Productions, and they're the parents of three adorable youngsters—Jenni, 7; Ami, 4; and Benji, one year old.

Herm Falk

Gail, the second member of the trio, came to us one night when the band was playing at the Palladium, in Hollywood. She cut in on me while I was having my usual tag dance with the ladies, and before she quite knew what was happening, she was onstage, singing with the band! When she finished, the applause was so great I knew we'd found another winner. A music major at the University of Tulsa, Gail has developed beautifully, singing, arranging, and playing piano solos for us.

   She's married to Rick Mallory, son of Mason and Ruth Mallory. (Mason is with Western Airlines, and we're old friends. He made arrangements for our Musical Family jaunt to Hawaii in 1972. In fact, that's how Gail met Rick—so *that's* keeping it all in the family, too!)

Tom Mareschal

And little Mary Lou Metzger is just so talented in so many ways, we depend on her for a dozen different functions. She not only sings well in the trio, but does perky little solos or duets with Jack Imel, is a terrific dancer, and a very fine actress. It's hard to find any fault with this young lady, who cooperates 100 percent, and is so reliable, so stable . . . and so pretty! I'm always secretly very proud of finding Mary Lou, because I had so much opposition when I first hired her. In fact, as I've mentioned in my other books, George Cates came storming into my office, complaining that he shouldn't be expected to work with "unprofessionals like that"! Today, George sings an entirely different tune . . . and is loudest of all in his praises of Mary Lou.

   Mary Lou is married to Richard Maloof, our bass and tuba player, and their wedding in 1973 was a happy occasion for all of us.

Tom Mareschal

Sandi was born August 1, in Northridge, California, and joined our Family in 1967; Gail was born October 6, in Salinas, California, and joined us in 1969; and Mary Lou was born November 13, in Philadelphia, Pennsylvania, and joined in 1970.

BOB RALSTON

Bob Ralston. What a genius. I'm so impressed with the way he plays that not long ago I decided to make an album with just Bob alone, on the Thomas organ . . . no band, just the simple beauty of the organ itself. Well, I want to tell you, folks, it wasn't easy! Musically, Bob and I don't always agree. But after a little hot and heavy discussion (during which I pointed out that *I* was the boss!), Bob agreed to do it my way, with no baubles, bangles, or birdcalls. And his musicianship was so superb, his interpretations of the songs so beautiful, I consider this recording to be one of the finest organ albums ever made.

I had the good sense to choose this young man as the winner of a talent contest when he was only fifteen years old. I didn't hire him then, but the moment he grew up—I hired him fast!

Bob lives with his family in the San Fernando Valley, and the Ralston household is rather an extensive one. Besides Bob's Dutch-born wife, Fietje, and their two children, Randy and Dianne, there are also a cat, a dog, a bird, a monkey—and a llama!

Bob was born July 2, in Montebello, California, and joined us in 1963.

KATHIE SULLIVAN

When I first heard Kathie Sullivan sing, I fell in love with the purity and brilliance of her voice, and tried to hire her on the spot. But she was just completing her studies at the University of Wisconsin and wanted to get her degree. So we compromised. Kathie sang with us till the following February, when our season ended, and then returned to the University to finish her schooling. Eight weeks later, when she returned to our show, she was armed with a Bachelor's Degree in Music.

We found her in Madison, Wisconsin, where she had been selected as the local Miss Champagne Lady. (On tour, our promoter, Lon Varnell, very often arranges a contest to find the best singer in the vicinity to serve as guest Champagne Lady.) Well, in Madison, Kathie won . . . naturally! . . . and as part of her duties, she met us at the plane that morning. On the drive into town she sang her winning song, "My Bill," for me, and I was so charmed I had her come right along with us and sing at all our scheduled appearances that day, as well as on the show that night.

I predict a great future for this young lady with the silvery soprano voice. I think it is one of the greatest voices I have ever heard in my lifetime.

Kathie was born May 31, in Oshkosh, Wisconsin, and joined us in 1976.

Tom Mareschal

KEN DELO

Ken Delo is a triple-threat man who can sing, dance, act, "talk"—or do almost anything else you ask! He headed up his own variety show in Australia before coming to us (Arthur Duncan was on the same show for a while, incidentally), and Ken's varied talents have been of tremendous help to us. One of his most popular "acts" is to grab a mike and go right out into the audience to sing and chat with the folks. Everybody has such a good time it's hard to get Ken back onstage again!

He's married to beautiful, blonde Marilyn Delo, an ex-ballerina, and they're the parents of two children who look as if they belong in a painting—Kimberly, now eight, and young Kevin, who's just turned five. (You can see a picture of them in our "Families" section, later on in the book.) Ken and his beautiful family are a wonderful addition to ours.

Ken was born December 8, in Detroit, Michigan, and joined us in 1969.

Tom Mareschal

Here's Ken singing, while Richard Maloof plays a few "oompahs" on his tuba.

JACK IMEL

Maybe some of you remember the first time Jack Imel appeared on our show . . . bright, beaming, and fresh out of the Navy. (And I mean fresh!) Well, Jack has come a long way since then. From a happy-go-lucky dancer and marimba player, he has developed into a totally responsible, creative performer, who is also our assistant producer.

Jack is in complete charge of our road shows, and has such meticulously prepared stage directions it makes things easy for us as well as all the stagehands in the various theaters we play. I never have to worry about a thing when I know Jack is in charge!

I'm just so very proud of him. He developed so beautifully that he has become invaluable to us in all phases of our work.

Here you see Jack doing the popular "challenge" dance with Bobby and Arthur.

Jack was born June 9, in Portland, Indiana, and joined us in 1957.

SEMONSKI SISTERS

What a beautiful family—with six lovely daughters! I love the whole family.

When I first found these little girls, I had some opposition from some of my friends and co-workers who thought I was attempting the impossible, trying to train unprofessional youngsters for the show. But I'm a stubborn German and I never give up on a project once I start! So I stuck with them, even though there were a few weeks in the beginning when I was afraid my critics were right! But before long the girls had learned how to really work, and today, they're wonderful examples of how well our training and sharing system operates. I'm just so proud of all of them.

They're as different as snowflakes . . . Donna, at 19, is the "worrier," the one who's so concerned that they all do the best possible job. JoAnne, 17, is the "moody" one; Valerie, 15, the "peacemaker"; Audrey, 14, the "shy" one; and Michelle, the baby, at nine and a half, the ham of the family. This little girl just loves to perform! (Diane, the eldest, left the group to concentrate on a song-writing career, and we all wish her the very best.)

Bill Harris

This was taken at Escondido when the girls first started on our training program. Left to right are: Michelle, JoAnne, Donna, Valerie, and Audrey, with Diane on guitar.

Donna was born April 20; JoAnne, July 23; Valerie, March 1; Audrey, March 28; and Michelle, August 16. All were born in New Jersey, and joined our show in 1974.

"Mama" Rusty is a fine singer, too, and a completely devoted, wonderful mother to her beautiful family. "Daddy" Joe is not only a sensational accordionist, but a dedicated father who fully understands his responsibilities to his daughters. In fact, these nice people were two of the main reasons I gambled on the girls. I knew, with parents like that, I couldn't go wrong!

Tom Mareschal

And here's the Band!

First, I'd like to have you meet our String Section:

Joe Livoti, our concertmaster. Joe heard Jascha Heifetz play when he was just a small boy in Boston, and was so inspired he wound up winning a scholarship to the Boston Conservatory of Music when he was only twelve, and another one.at fourteen! Joe, who's been with us twenty years, has an exceptionally beautiful tone, and great technique.

Tom Mareschal

Leo North

Bob Lido is our "specialty" man. He can play a hot violin in our Hotsy Totsy jazz group, fiddle up a storm in our country music hoedowns, or sing a rhythm song—all with equal skill. Bob has been with us twenty-four years and really comes to life when the spotlight hits him for a vocal! . . . **Harry Hyams** is one of the most highly regarded viola players in the nation. A graduate of the Juilliard School of Music, he's in constant demand to play with symphony orchestras, both here and in Europe. Here's Harry with his pride and joy, his boat, *Sarita*, on which he and his wife, Maya, spend much of their time.

A. H. Jacobs

Next, we have our wonderful Brass Section:

It's essential in a good band to have a strong lead trumpet man—strong enough, as the saying goes, to "carry the whole band." And **Mickey McMahon**, with his soaring powerful tone, more than fills the bill. Formerly with the Les Brown band, Mickey is a truly fine musician, completely dependable, absolutely reliable, and a real joy to have around.

I could say much the same thing about both **Laroon Holt** and **Charlie Parlato**. Laroon, who joined us four years ago, is another former child prodigy, who started playing at the age of five (early training again!) and played with the great Tommy Dorsey band when he was still a very young man.

Charlie Parlato, of the beaming and friendly face, is a very versatile performer. Charlie not only plays in our regular trumpet section, he also contributes a few hot licks to our Dixieland band, fits very well into our various choral groups, and, with his whimsical flair for comedy, adds a great deal to our comedy sketches too.

And finally, we have our "young man with a horn," **Johnny Zell**, who has such a dramatic and exciting style he never fails to bring forth a storm of applause from our audiences with his solos! I might add that Johnny is just as clean and fresh and nice as he looks in this picture, and his deep religious faith is an inspiration to us all.

And now the Trombones:

Leading off the Trombone Section is **Don Staples**, our clean-cut and smiling young man from Billings, Montana, who—quietly, capably, and unerringly—worked his way up to first trombone chair during the eleven years he's been with us. Totally dependable, absolutely dedicated, he's also one of the nicest people you'd ever want to meet . . . **Kenny Trimble** is another of those steady, dependable, top-flight artists so vital to any band. No matter what time I arrive for rehearsal—and I arrive early—Kenny is always there ahead of me. He and his wife, Bonnie, have a young grandson, Jason, who plans on joining the band someday. (He is already asking where he will sit. Now that's real foresight.)

Don Keck

Bob Havens, in my opinion, is the greatest Dixieland jazz trombone man in the nation. I really get my "kicks" when Bob starts playing! He was a great fan of the famed Jack Teagarden, and played with Al Hirt and Pete Fountain before coming to us, and his tremendous style and his complete control make his fellow musicians want to put down their own instruments and applaud. A great, great talent.

And finally, we come to **Barney Liddell!** Barney and I have had our moments during the almost thirty years we've been together (I can't believe it's been that long!) and there were times when I was ready to throw in the towel. But Barney, who is a truly great trombone man, is also one of the best-hearted, most generous people I've ever known, and he's not only worked hard to overcome a few roadblocks— he also works constantly for the betterment of the band, and himself, and today, we're pals. Here you see us "the way we were," back in the late forties when Barney joined us in Chicago, and again when we're celebrating his twenty-fifth year with the band by presenting him with a stereo radio.

And now meet the Reed Section!

I'm extremely proud of our Reed Section. **Dave Edwards**, our Alabama representative, who joined us in 1969, occupies first chair. Dave plays with such a mellow tone and such beautiful phrasing! But then every member of our reed section is outstanding (including, of course, Dick Dale and Henry Cuesta). I would say everyone in the reed section—well, the whole band, really—is dedicated to his profession and takes great pride in owning the finest instruments. And none more so than **Bob Davis**, who buys only the best, takes excellent care of them—and practices constantly! Bob, who's been with us since 1966, is our lead flutist . . . **Russ Klein** is such a fine musician, a complete professional, with extensive big-band experience, including several years with Freddie Martin. Russ has been with us for twenty years, and he's the one who blows those "hot licks" in our jazz combos. Responsible, reliable, and fun to be around, he has another claim to fame—in my eyes, anyway! He's married to my long-time secretary, Lois Lamont.

And now, here comes our Rhythm Section!

About a year or so ago, our long-time drummer, **Johnny Klein**, for health reasons decided he'd like to switch jobs and become our music librarian, and today, he's doing a wonderful job for us in this capacity. At first I was a little concerned over where we'd find a good drummer to replace him, but, as so often happens, the Good Lord took a hand in things—and **Paul Humphrey** walked into my life. Actually, he walked into my office and, after a little conversation, he said, "Mr. Welk, I'd like to become a member of your Musical Family." "Paul," I said, getting up and coming round the desk to shake his hand, "that's one of the greatest compliments I've ever received!" "Does that mean I've got the job?" he asked, smilingly. "It sure does," I said emphatically. Actually, I was delighted, because Paul is considered one of the super drummers in the business. And, after knowing him these past few months, I'd say he's a super man, too, a fine gentleman we're all proud to have with us.

Don Keck

Neil Levang, "Fiddling Neil," as he used to be called when he had his own radio show in Seattle, is a superb guitarist, in constant demand for recordings and motion pictures. I've seen Neil bring a huge audience to absolute silence with the purity and beauty of his guitar solos. A tremendous talent . . . And here's **Richard Maloof** with his beautiful bride, Mary Lou Metzger. Richard not only plays the string bass, he also plays the bass guitar and the tuba, and he's the one who puts all those "oom-pahs" in our fun and novelty numbers. A superlative musician . . .

Don Keck

Bob Smale was with us for two years before I discovered how good he was. Once I found out, I kept him so busy playing solos and specialty numbers that I finally apologized for working him so hard. "That's all right," said this quiet young man, "I love to work." He's a fine arranger, too, and many of the big-band arrangements you hear are Bob's. A real virtuoso, he has a music degree from the University of California.

And finally we come to our beloved **Larry Hooper**, who was so very ill for such a long time. Over six feet tall, Larry lost so much weight he got down to ninety pounds and was just skin and bones for long, worrisome months. But finally, with the help of prayers and medical skill, he began to recover, and we show him here on the day he came back to the studio for the first time . . . completely recovered and ready to work. I think you can see the joy in both our faces as we acknowledge the cheers and applause of the studio audience, who seem to be saying, "Welcome back, Larry!" In a way, Larry's story epitomizes the family feeling in the band. We all stuck by him during the four long years he was ill, and we welcomed him back with open arms when he returned and made our family complete once again.

And here are two of the most important members of all in our Musical Family. One you see on camera every week — and one you never see. But both are absolutely indispensable to the show, and both — in my opinion — are geniuses.

JIM HOBSON

First our producer-director, **Jim Hobson**. Jim has worked with me for over twenty-five years, and I'm constantly amazed that anyone can be as full of creative ideas as he is! All I have to do is suggest a song, or a theme for a show . . . and before I get the words out of my mouth, he's come up with a dozen different ways to stage it! He just spouts over with ideas and visions.

Jim is solely responsible for getting the show on the air, and for keeping it moving, and he does a superlative job. In fact, I consider him the finest director for a musical show in television, without question.

The only thing that bugs me about Jim is that he never looks a day older! With his cashmere sweater pulled over a white shirt, he still looks like a Harvard undergraduate.

He has many wonderful qualities, far too many for me to enumerate here, but I'd say the greatest is his ability to correct our performers—and have them love him for it! He has the gift of communication—and his genuine niceness is one of the greatest assets we have on the show.

Don Keck

GEORGE CATES

And now our Musical Director, George Cates. What a great talent. George is a truly brilliant man in many ways, and when it comes to music—he's a genius! He's been of tremendous help, not only to me but to the entire orchestra, and the band is much better today because of him.

I wouldn't say George is exactly the quiet type. On the contrary, he's been known to raise his voice! But that's only because he's so fiercely dedicated to the betterment of the show.

Our backgrounds are very different. He's a city boy from New York, with a host of musical degrees, while I'm a farm boy from North Dakota, with none. (I "learned by doing"!) But we have a wonderful rapport and work together very easily, because we're exactly alike in our devotion to the orchestra. Both of us are totally concerned with pleasing our audience.

(One little sidelight on George: A few years ago, I suggested he assist me by conducting the band on camera. Well, he took to it like a duck to water! "George," I said, "I've worked with you for twenty-five years. But this is the first time I ever knew you were a ham!")

George Cates

Behind the Scenes

Behind the lights and costumes and glamor
are some very hard-working folks who make
it all happen. And here are some of the talented
people who help make our "stars" shine.

Rose Weiss has been our costume designer since the inception of the show—and we all love her! She cares as much as I do about every little detail, and frets and worries over color schemes and costumes till she gets everything exactly right. Here we're hugging each other at birthday time. (That's Tanya beaming at us.)

Leo North

Bob Ballard, whom you see playing the piano in the picture on the opposite page, is our chief arranger, and he's just about perfect for our band. It was no surprise to me when he was elected vice-president of the American Society of Music Arrangers, because he not only does a super job for the band, he also directs our choral group, and is chiefly responsible for the Semonski Sisters' "sound," too. A man of great intellectual stability, Bob's advice is invariably sensible, practical— and invaluable! He's done a tremendous job of improving the quality and scope of the orchestra, and all of us hold him in the highest esteem.

Joe Rizzo is everybody's favorite, the kind of man who just loves his work and is willing to help anyone who needs it. He's just as talented as he is nice—and that's pretty talented—and many of the fine arrangements you hear the band play on our show come from his brilliant imagination.

And **Curt Ramsey** used to play in our trumpet section, but he had such a wide and thoroughgoing knowledge of music, I recruited him to be our chief music librarian. Mention a song to Curt, and if he doesn't know who wrote it and when, he knows exactly where to find it! You also see him singing in our quintets and trios from time to time. Curt does a wonderful job.

George Thow, a quiet, soft-spoken Scotsman, is a walking encyclopedia of information about the big-band era. Formerly with the Dorsey Brothers, Isham Jones, and Jack Teagarden, among others, George played jazz trumpet for us for a while, too. But when I discovered he was a Harvard graduate with a degree in French and a flair for writing, I took him away from the band and assigned him the task of watching over my vocabulary. "With my four years of schooling," I told him, "I'm apt to say the wrong thing—and lose us the whole show!" So now I depend on George's good taste to keep me out of trouble. And we all depend on him for his enormous expertise in the music field, to help us write and produce the show.

Don Keck

Doug Smart, our associate director, is Jim Hobson's find, a "smart" young man whose youth is a great asset to us. His knowledge of today's music keeps us in tune with what's happening. (He's a good drummer, too!)

Leo North

Charles Koon is the genius who designs all those lovely sets you see on the show. And that's not just my opinion. He's worked for twenty years with Jim Hobson, who says, flatly . . . "The man's a genius!"

Celebrations

In every family there are highs and
lows, joys and sorrows,
bad times and good. And it's the
same in our Musical Family,
although I must say that the good has
far outweighed the bad.
Here are some of our happiest moments,
our celebrations, our joys —
with maybe just one or two low spots!

This was certainly a high spot, landing on the cover of a national magazine in 1957. That's Barney with me, and the late Pete Lofthouse in the background.

EXCLUSIVE! NASSER TELLS WHY HE'S ANTI-AMERICAN

LOOK

15¢ JUNE 25, 1957

LAWRENCE WELK

Nobody likes him but the public

Courtesy Barney Liddell

All those pretty girls surrounding me make my birthday a little easier
to take. In fact, it makes me feel younger!

Here I am walking across the sands beside the ruins of the old Aragon
Ballroom on Lick Pier in Santa Monica, which burned to the ground in
1970. A great many wonderful memories went up in smoke that night.

Los Angeles *Times*

Well, at least Fern likes it! And so did Sam Lutz, and Mason Mallory of Western Airlines, whom you see in white shirts in the background. But as you can see, it was too much for me!

Ron Edmonds, Honolulu *Star Bulletin*

And they call this work!

A milestone, a real turning point for us. Tanya and I are holding a map of our first syndicated network, the stations that joined us after we were canceled by ABC. All those dots represent the cities that made up our initial network. Today we have 228 stations in the United States, and 31 in Canada.

Every year on the Christmas show, our production staff lets me sing one line from *Jingle Bells*, " . . . what fun it is to ride and sing a sleighing song tonight." I forgot the words, and as you can see, it broke us all up, Mary Lou, Gail, and myself.

An honorary "doctor," Doctor of Music, from North Dakota State University.

Sam Lutz and his wife, Irene, and our wonderful sponsor and dear friend, Ed Kletter of the J. B. Williams Company, who accompanied Fern and me to Hawaii when I appeared on behalf of the Cancer Society there. That's one of my favorite charities and I've been chairman or co-chairman three times.

That's little Lawrence Welk the Third ("Buns," to his friends), and you can see little Jenni Griffiths beside him.

Mike Arnold

In the annual Hollywood Santa Claus Parade. The third time I've paraded down that happy boulevard.

With Michelle Semonski. This little girl has everything going for her . . . talent, youth, a happy disposition—and a close and loving family.

Wedding Days

Weddings are "high spots" in any family, and
we've certainly had our share.
Here are some pictures that bring back
happy memories not only of our
beautiful weddings, but of some other
very joyous occasions, too.

Here's Sandi and Brent Griffiths cutting their wedding cake at their
reception at the Church of Jesus Christ of Latter Day Saints in Granada Hills.

Roy Griffiths

Walter Zurlinden

Here are Richard
and Mary Lou Metzger Maloof,
just after walking down the aisle
of St. Charles Church, in North
Hollywood, California, and out
into the sunshine as Mr. and Mrs.!

Curl Ray Studio, Long Beach, CA

Bobby and Kristie Burgess at the altar of Our Saviour's Lutheran Church in Long Beach, California, just after their wedding on Valentine's Day in 1971. All the bridesmaids wore red velvet gowns to carry out the Valentine theme, and Kristie's sentimental daddy, Myron Floren, cried all through the ceremony. (From happiness, I might add!)

And Gail Farrell and her brand-new husband, Rick Mallory, at the altar of the Westwood Hills Christian Church, in Westwood, California, just moments after their beautiful wedding!

Walter Zurlinden

My lovely daughter-in-law, Tanya, and my proud and happy son, Larry Welk, Jr.

This was taken in Medora, North Dakota, during a Fourth of July parade. Aren't those North Dakotans wonderful, friendly folks? No wonder I love to go home!

Courtesy Harold Schafer

What a lucky man I am to have "high spots" like this, week after week!
I just love to visit with the folks in the studio audience before we tape our
show every Tuesday, and here I am at dress rehearsal doing the polka
with one of the nice ladies from the audience.

Bill Harris

Leo North

Don't these little girls welcoming Fern and me to Hawaii have lovely smiles? I don't know who's smiling harder, the girls or us!

Leo North

We thoroughly enjoyed our location trip to Hawaii, as you can see by
the way we're making short work of these "goodies"!

Happy Thanksgiving! Here, Norma Zimmer and Jimmy Roberts act as "mother and father" during our annual Thanksgiving Day program. We truly are grateful for our many blessings.

Leo North

Merry Christmas!

Leo North

And a Happy New Year!

Leo North

Happy Days

Some days stick out in your mind as especially happy, simply because you're with people you love, working or playing together. And here are some of our happiest.

I like this picture. Brings back memories of moonlight hayrides and barn dances! Left to right are: Ken, Anacani, Bobby, Joe, Jimmy, Guy, and Tom. In front are: Cissy, Sandi, Gail, Ralna, and Mary Lou.

Bill Harris

What a tough life I lead!

Tom Mareschal

Gail is a gypsy, Dick looks as if he just got off a Mississippi River
showboat, and I'm not sure just what Mary Lou is supposed to be.
But don't they look nice?

I bought this baby accordion years ago for my son, Larry. He didn't take to it—so now I'm trying with my grandchildren. (So far, no takers!)

Here I am with the band at the University of North Dakota, where I was guest professor for a day. I even lectured to the students (but I did better leading the band).

Aren't they brave? Sandi, Mary Lou, and Gail had great fun feeding this baby rhino at the San Diego Children's Zoo.

Leo North

Aren't they lovely? We are all so very, very proud of our lovely ladies, because that's exactly what they are . . . lovely—and ladies.

Here I am doing the light fantastic with a couple of elephants. If I'd known some of the things I'd have to do in this business, I might never have left the farm! This was taken to publicize our record hit, "Baby Elephant Walk."

The boys and I getting together on the kind of music I love best—
Dixieland!

Tom Mareschal

Holding hands and thanking God for the privilege of having spent a
happy year together, and looking forward to another "wunnerful" year
ahead.

Isn't she a cuddler? We're all laughing because I just asked this lovely lady from the studio audience what kept her so young and pretty, and she said, "Well, I just do what you tell me—take Geritol!" (My sponsors liked that!)

Here I am with three of the most beautiful girls in the world, Sandi, Ralna and Gail. This is the way our girls looked in one of our opening acts at Harrah's in Lake Tahoe, as they each stepped through a portal to the strains of "The Most Beautiful Girl in the World"!

I don't remember just what the joke was—but aren't we having fun?

Once a year my manager Sam Lutz calls me and says, "Well, Lawrence, it's that time again, time for new publicity pictures." So here I am, waving my baton for the camera (and wishing I were out on the golf course).

We really mean it when we sing of our love for our flag and our country.
It's the best in the world.

Dancing with lovely ladies is
part of my "work." And do I love it!

Our Musical Family's Families

What's a family without children?
Or mothers and daddies — or grandmas
and grandpas? That's what *makes* a family —
and I'd like you to meet some of ours.

Dunlap-Turney Photography, Glendale, CA

Sandi Griffiths and her baby son, Benji. Isn't she beautiful? And isn't this a beautiful picture? No wonder it won a Merit Award in the national exhibition of the Professional Photographers of America, for photographer Ron Brown. To my mind, it catches all the beauty, tenderness, and love of motherhood.

Here's the rest of
Sandi's family: husband,
Brent Griffiths, at rear,
with daughters Ami and Jenni
in front, and little Benji,
now one year old, beaming
up at me. Looks like
he's asking for an audition!

Ken Delo doesn't really need to read the name tags
to tell him who these children are, because one is his
pretty daughter, Kimberly, and the other is
handsome son, Kevin.

Here's Producer Jim Hobson, with his pretty wife, Elsie, snapped as they were flying to Hawaii for our big "special." Elsie used to be an actress; in fact, she met Jim when both were fellow students at the Pasadena Playhouse.

Leo North

There's the llama I told you about in the Bob Ralston family! Left to right are: Bob's son, Randy, holding the family cat, Mew; Bob, with the llama, Noël; wife, Fietje, holding Charlie, the dog; and little Dianne, with the family monkey, Laura!

Don Keck

The Paul Humphrey family:
wife, Joan, and daughter, Pier,
just days before son, Damien,
was born!

Tom Mareschal

Little Pier Humphrey, dancing on our Christmas show.
Her teacher was dancing right along with her, just outside
of our camera range, and when the dance was over and
the studio audience burst into applause, Pier's eyes lit up
like Christmas candles!

Here are Guy and Ralna with their parents, Mr. and Mrs. Guy Hovis and Mr. and Mrs. Raul English. "There's been a succession of Guy Hovises in our family for generations, and I'm proud to carry on the name," says our Guy. Ralna's equally close to her family. It makes my heart overflow to see the great love our kids have for their own families. No wonder our Musical Family is so rich in love.

Tom Mareschal

Tom Mareschal

And here's Henry Cuesta and his beautiful family: wife, Janette; daughters, Marion and Lucinda; and son, Henry, Jr.

Lee Rodriguez Photography, Houston, Texas

Meet Miss Becki Jane Burgess, who made her debut on November 17, 1976.

And here's the whole Burgess family: Kristie, Bobby, and Becki. (Kristie made those matching green-and-white outfits herself!)

Keys Studios, Hollywood

Bob Smale; his pretty wife, Mary; daughter, Margaret; and son, Robbie.

Mickey McMahon and wife, LaDean,
having fun on a trip.

Looks like Grandma is ready to defend the whole tribe! Here are Don Staples; wife, Betty; daughters, Sheryl and Debbie; and grandma, Florence Briese!

Laroon Holt and his happy family: wife, Claudene; son, Tim; daughter, Heidi.

And Dave Edwards and his pretty wife, Phyllis; sons, David and Charles.

Don Mazer Photography, Woodland Hills, CA

You might not think it to look at him, but Jack Imel is not only a papa—
he's a "grandpapa"—and here's proof. In front row are his
daughter Cindy and son Terry; middle row, Timothy,
Debbie, Jack, and son Greg, holding grandson, Larry.
In top row are Kevin Gaspar (Debbie's husband), and
Jack's wife, Norma.

Our concertmaster, Joe Livoti, and his lovely wife, Irma.

Dick and Marguerite Dale and their nice family, as they looked on their
Christmas card: David, Danny, Deedee, Rick, and Bambi, the dog!

Bob Plunkett

George Cates

George Cates took this picture of himself
and his beautiful wife, Miriam, all by himself.
Don't ask me how, I told you he was a genius!

Here's Roger Sullivan, accompanying his wife, Ava Barber, on the drums.

Don Keck

Charlie Parlato and his talented sons, David and Christopher. (That's David on the bass fiddle.)

Johnny Zell with his pretty little daughter, Lisa, and son, John, Jr.

Bob Havens and his beautiful bride, Constance.

Here's Gail Farrell and her handsome husband, Rick Mallory, looking happy together.

Anacani and her lovely "mama," chatting with our studio audience.

Here's Ken Delo singing to his lovely wife, Marilyn.

Don Keck

Norma's husband, Randy, had been told he'd be on crutches for the rest of his life, but prayers and medical treatment worked miracles. And here they are celebrating—by dancing!

Part of the "Family," Too

These people are so close
to my heart I consider them
part of the "family," too.

Eddie Shipstad

Here I am on the golf course at Tahoe with some of my dearest friends and business associates. (Left to right are: Irving Ross; Matty Rosenhaus; Senator John Harmer; Eddie Shipstad; my managers, Sam Lutz and Don Fedderson; me; and Eddie's brother, Roy.

I can't let this opportunity pass without saying something about my sponsor, Matty Rosenhaus of the J. B. Williams Company. I feel so very fortunate to be associated with him. More than a sponsor, more than a businessman, he is my friend—and a treasured one. On the evening of the day that ABC canceled us, he called me from Florida with words I'll never forget. "Lawrence," he said, "we just heard the bad news and I just want to tell you that no matter what route you and the band decide to take—we want to go with you. We still believe in you." I honestly feel that Matty's affectionate and loyal support has been a big factor in keeping us on the air, and we are so grateful we try constantly to do the best shows we possibly can to justify his faith in us.

Devoted to his beautiful wife, Gila, and their three lovely children, Sarita, Loretta, and Hedy, Matty's own standards elevate ours, and he is loved and respected by every member of our "family."

One other nice thing about Matty: he's as sentimental as I am! But if you see us crying, don't worry—chances are they're just tears of happiness!

Escondido. Isn't this lovely? Do you blame me for sneaking down there as often as I can? Escondido is an oasis in my busy life.

When you dine in the restaurant at our place in Escondido, you get a good view of the lake marking the center of the eighteen-hole golf course which winds through the park. Until recently, the "champagne glass" fountain in the center of the lake was the big attraction . . . but now it's these baby ducks! They were a big surprise because all of us had assumed the two big ducks which had been swimming around were both male. Well, obviously, one of them wasn't! And when these little fellows were born, you never saw such excitement. They're now the pets of the whole place.

Doug Smart

Fern and I sampling the buffet at the regular brunch served every Sunday at our Escondido restaurant, while our fine manager, Paul Ryan, and "super chef," Bill Balnaves, make sure the "bosses" are pleased!

Eddie Shipstad

My secretary, Lois Lamont. Lois joined us right out of high school in 1945, and has been with us ever since. She had very little training but, as the band grew, so did she, and over the years has come up with so many innovations, and so many more efficient ways to run the business, that today she's more than my secretary—she's an officer in the company.

Lois suffered some serious health problems about three years ago, and we all worried about her. But last spring she and her husband, Russ Klein, took off on a five-week air-and-sea tour from Japan to Bali, and Sumatra to Singapore—a very grueling trip. There were forty-two passengers in the group, and every single one of them got sick—except Lois! That made us all happy. I just can't say enough nice things about this lovely, loyal lady, whose dedication to the band is unmatched.

I thought I'd put Ted Lennon here among our Escondido pictures because he's done so much in the past few years to make this resort a heavenly place. Ted has developed so beautifully since I hired him as a talent scout twenty years ago, and become so expert at his job, that today he is executive vice-president of our corporation. His good judgment, brilliant head for business (and Irish sense of humor) make him one of my most valued and trusted advisors. He's an uncle of the famed Lennon Sisters, by the way, and his brother, Jack, is also an important member of our business family.

Del-Hagen Studio, Santa Monica, CA

This fine gentleman is one of my dearest friends, Lon Varnell, one of the most wonderful people God ever put on this earth. Lon takes us on tour twice a year, and he's so perfect at what he does he's ruined me for anybody else! I love to have philosophical discussions with him, partly because he's a fountainhead of wisdom—and partly because he has such a delightful Southern accent! Here we are in Hawaii, where Lon took us all on a personal-appearance tour in 1972.

Here I am on another favorite golf course, the Indian Wells Country Club, near Palm Springs, with John Curci. Twenty-one of the nice folks at the club presented me with this golf cart. We have a home there, and every year some of my Musical Family and I attend their annual Pow-Wow party. It's always lots of fun.

Here are my managers, Sam Lutz and Don Fedderson. Oh, you can't see them? Well, when Don realized he was out of camera range, he promptly stuck a hand in front of Sam's face, so he'd be out of range, too! (They're just kidding, folks; they're really great friends.)

Handsome Bob Warren has announced our television show since 1960, and he's terrific at warming up the audience before the show. (He's also pretty good at dancing with the ladies!)

Byron Nelson, one of the world's greatest golfers, has been such a wonderful help to me with my golf game, that we're all grateful to him! In fact, we'd like to make this fine gentleman an honorary "member of the family"!

Eddie Shipstad

Here are Eddie Shipstad and me surrounded by our grandchildren!
Eddie, who originated the famous Ice Follies, took several of the
pictures in this book. He's my golfing pal, and he and his wife, Lu, are
our very dear friends.

Christine and David,
Donna's children,
getting some ice cream from Grandpa,
just before
we took off for Hawaii.

Macy Roger Du Row

My little granddaughter Christine and I.
She's getting a big hug from Grandpa
because she just played such a nice
piano solo on our Christmas show.

Our lovely Shirley and her brood. Husband Bob is holding Lisa, then Jonathan, Shirley, David, Laura, and Robbie.

And here's the lady who's responsible for the whole thing, my lovely wife, Fern.

When we were young! Shirley, Larry, Donna, and I, ready for a bike ride in River Forest, Illinois.

And here he is . . . Lawrence Welk the Third!

Eddie Shipstad

This was taken on Mother's Day, May 1977, after dinner at the Bel Air
Country Club in Los Angeles, with our whole family present except for
our eldest granddaughter, Laura, Shirley's daughter.

Back row, left to right: Shirley's husband, Bob; sons David and
Robbie; Donna's son Jimmy; Shirley's Jonathan; Donna's husband,
James; and our son, Larry Welk, Jr.

Middle row, left to right: Shirley's youngest, Lisa; then Christine
(Donna's); then Lawrence Welk the Third, and brother, Kevin; and
Donna's youngest, David.

Front row: I'm in front with Donna, then Fern, then Shirley and Tanya.
Doesn't Fern look like a queen? I am so grateful to her for the beautiful,
beautiful family she has given me. We all love her.

And here we are, all together, at the annual dinner party Bill Harrah
gives for us in his beautiful home in Lake Tahoe. This was taken on
July 1, 1977. What a wonderful group of friends! What a wonderful
"family"! And what a lucky man I am. Front row, left to right: Mr. and
Mrs. Bob Ring, Mr. and Mrs. Sam Lutz, Fern and I, Mr. and Mrs. Bill Harrah.

Throughout this book, I have tried to convey the depth of my feelings about the importance of family life. You've seen pictures and little stories about my Musical Family, their families, and now, my family. And I must confess that without Fern, we wouldn't have had a family life. She is the one who has held us together, the one who has given so unstintingly of her love and devotion that she would have willingly given her life at any time for any of our children. No wonder they all adore her! She has given us a home that will live in our hearts forever.

I love my family deeply and devotedly, but in the life I've chosen . . . the one the Good Lord has seen fit to give me . . . I've had another family, too—my Musical Family—whom I love, and want to help and guide as much as I do my own.

And I'm a very lucky man. Because of Fern, I've been able to work in the larger world of the Musical Family and the nation itself, bringing as much joy and happiness as we possibly can. And—also because of Fern—I have a family of my own, too. I have love in the home. And nothing—no glory, no fame, nor worldly success—can surpass that.

It is something I would wish for all of you.

Benarie